Immaculate
Fuel

Previously published:

Rogue Apostle

Immaculate Fuel

Mary Jane Nealon

Four Way Books
New York City

Distributed by
University Press of New England
Hanover and London

Editorial Office
Four Way Books
POB 535, Village Station
New York, NY 10014
www.fourwaybooks.com

Library of Congress Catalogue Card Number: 2002116854

ISBN: 1-884800-53-X

Cover art: *Christ Entering Puberty*, by Sherri Kirlin.
By permission of the collector.

This book is manufactured in the United States of America
and printed on acid-free paper.

Four Way Books is a division of Friends of Writers, Inc.,
a Vermont-based not-for-profit organization. We are grateful
for the assistance we receive from individual donors and
private foundations.

Distributed by University Press of New England
One Court Street, Lebanon, NH 03766

ACKNOWLEDGMENTS

Thank you to the editors of the following magazines:

Heliotrope: "Ritual, My Father"

Hanging Loose: "Flop House," and "Human-Headed Bull Below Empty Space"

The Cream City Review: "Attachment"

The Rio Grande Review: "Commuting," "Easter," and "Shames, Also Love"

Forklift, Ohio: "Moon Landing, 1969"

Grateful acknowledgment to The Fine Arts Work Center
in Provincetown, The New Jersey State Council on the Arts,
and The Mid-Atlantic Arts Foundation for their generous support.
Thanks to Martha Rhodes for all editing suggestions, and for
confidence in the work. Thanks to all the mentors, old and new,
among them: Joan Aleshire, Steve Orlen, Dan Tobin, and Sandra
Alcosser. And finally, with gratitude to Ellen Bryant Voigt who
guided me through two years of loss with the excitement of study.

For Cathy and Mike, with love.

In memory of my parents.

CONTENTS

I

MOON LANDING, 1969

It starts to rain, and my blue
Schwinn is tilting
in the mud. *You have time,*
my father says, *the rain will ruin your bike.*

My family is a circle of silhouettes
before the gray TV light. I'm alone in the rain
with my bike. There's salt

water in the air. I taste it.
I watch the moon from the yard.
Shouts from the houses.

Fireworks like gunshots
release their sparks
over Shark River. I stay in the yard,

poised between the mundane
and the extraordinary. I am 13 years old,
in a navy blue bathing suit,

leaning on a kickstand, thinking
that soon I'll be missed
and will have to huddle with all the excited

neighbors and strangers, but for a moment
I am watching the moon, and the smoky
sky around it,

feeling something large taken from me,
like a wing, or a lung.

RAPTURE

On the rocks this morning an elephant seal gives birth.
Blue head and smashing pink fluid.
Everything begins in violence, a bystander says.
The autistic says, *waves, there's waves, there's lots and lots of waves.*

≈

I held an eleven-year-old girl in my arms. The hospital had bad
linoleum, curled and sharp. We were in a ten-bed ward, stench
    of old blood and afterbirth.
The girl, raped in the Duncan Projects, described being upside
down on the metal stairs, and a ripping.
I held her as she gave birth to his baby: a stillborn with two heads –
one tiny undeveloped head arising from the neck of the true baby.

≈

My father saw a crime in everybody.
Suspicion was a kind of wildflower for him.

≈

My brother said he saw Jesus before he died,
but then again, he was trying to find ways to reassure us.

≈

I saw a boy in New Mexico.
I saw him on a gurney and he was stunningly
handsome, the back of his head had been shot away
and it was my job to keep it packed with gauze
while we waited for his family to say *yes*
to his heart, his kidneys, his skin.

≈

Sometimes when we make love
and I am upside down in bed
or I am cupping your head in my lap,
I remember the girl with the baby,
I remember the handsome boy.

≈

My father told me that once, on Brunswick Street, a freight train
headed for Secaucus crashed and a bull broke free.
It ran past the Lorillard Shoe Factory, past Tony's vegetable stand and Juan's
bodega. It crushed Mr. Capezolli's roses, and then turned on the street filling
with people, and raced towards Monk Donoghue's mother and speared her
        against a car.
You have to be prepared for things you could never imagine,
my father said. But remember, suspicion was a wildflower for him,
was a beautiful weapon against surprise.

≈

When my brother's heart monitor went flat
Jesus was a greeting card in the room.
My father was unwavering in a blue sweater; I thrust
my face into the wool of it. He was *immovable,*
but he had been preparing his whole life for catastrophe.

≈

My friends sometimes ask me to tell stories about people dying.
I've never seen anyone die badly, I tell them.
Everyone is always peaceful, I say.
The autistic says, *waves, there's waves, there's lots and lots of waves.*

COMMUTING

At the narrow entrance to Little West 12th Street, a man appears,
holding a cup mid-air. He doesn't drag his paralyzed right leg,
but swings it out, in perfectly repeated arcs,
using all his hip strength, keeping pace with his good side
which he moves swiftly and with confidence. He is not begging us.
He barely pauses at each car. Around his neck hangs a sign:
Out of Work, it says. His leg, like an insect's jointed pattern,
shadows out and away, springs back
and forth and back. A metronome of a walk.
All day I drag myself from task to task, ordinary day in a year
when both my parents died. My mother rested her hand
on my head, said, *you're such a good girl,*
and months later, my father said, *I don't want to be too sleepy,*
I want to see how I handle it. This is the arc of my body.
I swing it efficiently through the day. But I am, unlike the stranger,
without grace. I am stunned, tepid, orphaned.
The stoplight finally changes; I go towards it,
and see, in my mirror, his back,
and the sign's other side: *Out of Home,* it says.

NIGHT SHIFT

The doors make their soft electric *ppfiff* open,
a man comes in, carried by his hysterical sons,
blood all over his chest,
blood drips onto the floor, where the sons slip
and try to keep him swinging like a hammock
between them. His head hits the gurney
as they lift him up, the way you might toss a small child, in an arc,
    above a lake.
We know it is impossible to save him.
Get out – we push his sons through the door,
count the number of tears in his skin.
We need time to get a chest tube in, time
to enter his drowned throat,
and it is just the two of us here, furious
with his sons. By not calling an ambulance,
they have doomed him,
given him over to us,
without equipment, without the necessary skill.

It is nearly 6 AM when we officially give up.
My arms and legs cramp from trying to save him.
Alone behind the curtain with his body, I think:
what if we had just stopped for a moment and called out his name?
    Pablo Chonto, your crucifix is knotted in your chest hair.
    Outside, the pacing bodies of your sons,
    so much like you: wide backs, hair to their shoulders...
I pour peroxide over him and it steams, it froths
and bubbles in the blood, which I wipe clean,
exposing knife thrusts. I wipe this man's face,
then clean spilled shit from his thighs.
I mourn Pablo, whom I didn't know 2 hours ago,
and forgive his weeping sons.

FLOPHOUSE

Can Delmore die?
        – John Berryman

In hotels above restaurant supply stores
and shops with gorgeous lighting fixtures,
where people pause to *ooh* and *aah*,
the men are in their stalls.

I visit, pretend it is about their health,
take a blood pressure, or dress a gaping sore.
Some men are veterans,
some are drunks, some are still at war.

When one dies, EMS takes him
down the stairs, the clerk fumigates
and sweeps, and within hours, another man
has tied his shoes to hooks or rigged

a lamp for reading. *Of course,*
I would tell Berryman,
he could die. The men die all the time.
When Delmore died, alone in his hotel

the blood, they said, was *streaming,*
another was waiting for his stall
who would find some sign of *poet:*
an object in a locker, a word taped to the wall.

THE PRIESTHOOD

I.

I thought I'd be a priest
or an Indian Saint like Kateri Tekawitha –
she survived smallpox with blinded eyes and a disfigured face.
The book about her was the first thing I stole.

I took a chunk of fudge and gave it to my brother.
I wanted to be *heroic*. Caught,
I was forced to tell Father Griffith, but in the confessional,
I wanted to be the powerful one, not the sinner on the other side.
I made a private vow.

Pope Paul the VI appeared on the steps of St. Pat's.
The crowd screened, swooned.
Blessings flew in the air. I thought I was seeing Jesus
and nearly fainted from hysteria.
My mother pointed to the Pope,
He's just a priest, she said, to calm me.

I wanted to be a priest: person in charge of ceremony,
magician of body and blood,
absolver of thieves like me.

My brother discovered a tumor. *Grapefruit*
they said. As though a tangy comparison could calm us.
I stole many things that year: the useless scapula
on my brother's bedpost. Fishnet stockings.
A change purse: small and green and leather
with a hammered rose. My stealing embarrassed the family.

Every Wednesday I was sent to after-school confession
for bad kids and adulterous wives. My priest idols
tilted their heads towards me,

whispering delicious forgivenesses.
Remember, my mother told me, *a priest is just a man.*

When my brother was nineteen, God suddenly swirled
in the invisible, an *idea.*
My mother's hand lingered on my back at my brother's deathbed.
She turned away from the final moment.
Everyone but us in the hallway when the clotted blood left his pelvis,
flew from the nest of his beloved lower belly,
and traveled to his heart. There in the room above the river,
he stared at me, breathless and afraid. His ribs,
like the hull of a boat, bowed out. And I in my fantasy
laid my hand on his forehead and told him how to go.
Convinced him of the way to go. Blessed him with my secret
priestness. Between us, the idea of God took shape.
This skin-to-skin pressure in the face of death's fluent body.
My mother's hand to my back while she looked out the window.

II.

Before my mother died
she lifted her arms so fast
she hit me in the face.
She was trying to *throw* her arms around me,
did throw them,
heavy as they were for her
who could no longer lift them.

When she did die, at 3 in the morning, I had fallen asleep,
my head on her knees, her hand on my head.
All the others were in their rooms, restless or dreaming.
I woke to her breath giving out, woke to her hands reclaiming my
        brother,
to her turning back from the window in the room where he had died,
turning finally to face him. And I left them there.

My hand on his forehead, her hand on my hair.
I am a keeper of things that don't belong to me.

The truth is, the Jesuits brought smallpox to the Indians.
They brought the need for conversion: fear
in the face of the epidemic. And Kateri Tekawitha,
scarred and made unbeautiful, wanted to be near them. Knew
that they would touch her, as they touched all the disfigured
and unpure, just as I knew
that the clap of the priest's incense holder released more
than the musky scent of God.

ABSOLUTION

"I dream of an ideal confessor to tell everything to, spill it all:
I dream of a blasé saint." – E.M. Cioran

I don't discuss impure thoughts and acts.
I want forgiveness for small abandonments:
my brother left alone after surgery to tie his own shoes.
My saint, apathetic, sits on a rock near me,
his gown falls between worn knees. He yawns,
he's seen worse: men drawn and quartered, women
burned at the stake. And then I leave him, even.

Infidelity, a gift I learn well.
I cheat on myself with myself,
confess my mixed emotions for the human body,
for the way I stand by and watch things happen.
For invasions, large and small: thin needles, chest tubes.
I watch primitive rituals and call them science.
I search the faces of the dead for answers –
Where have they gone to? Why are they cold?

My saint, meanwhile, signals me.
It's easy at the bedside of the suffering.
I'm good at what I do. But my sin is this:
I use the dying to understand where my brother has gone.
Each time I touch them I am studying their bodies
for clues. And the little prayers I say are always for myself.

II

DISCOVERY

Anthony Hewish makes a new telescope.
He has torn socks, licks postage stamps,
boils eggs until their white skins crack.
He has a dreamy mind.
A mind like a quick storm. A mustang mind.
The new telescope is wire and thousands of dipole antennas.
He transforms a field.

Jocelyn Bell comes from Belfast to help.
She monitors pulses from outer space.
A chair in hay, four hundred feet of print-outs flow from her lap.
She is studying sound. The paper like folds of vestments around her.
She is counting pings in a chair in high grass.
Antennas, like soldiers, are silhouettes that split the land.

> I am eleven years old.
> I make little altars to St. Theresa of the Roses.
> Recordo Ortero thrusts his hand up my navy blue uniform,
> my rosary beads like little weapons in my hands.
> I am dreaming of *out there* just like they are.

December 1967. A pear splits in a wood bowl,
Hewish uses its body to explain a star.
The pings are coming in perfectly spaced arcs.
Outside the solar system, inside the galaxy, over the field of antenna.
Secretly, they call the project *Little Green Men*.
He and Jocelyn are lovers only in the sense that they watch each other
from behind the telescope, in that they bend back the same distance,
in that they love the absence of ground light,
for the dramatic backdrop it makes.

> Once, a rat ran into the vestibule of our house.
> My father chased it with an ice chopper, and caught it,

and cleaved its squealing body. I had jumped onto the dining
    room table,
I fainted and fell and knocked out two teeth.
In the afterwards, ice pressed to the bloody lower lip,
I tried to recreate the deliciousness of fainting.

When all the discovering is done, and there are no green men
calling out to us, but merely the spinning neutron stars
of violent supernova explosions, Hewish admits that the weeks
before knowing were the most exciting of his life.

I make altars to the martyrs, and re-live my single
fainting spell as an ecstatic calling.

In 1054, Yang Wei-Te, a court astronomer, writes of a chaotic
    night sky.
That same year in a Northern Arizona desert, an Indian records a blazing
night, recreating a firefall. In nine centuries the stars will call out,
in perfectly repeated arcs, to an old English man and his eager
    graduate student.
The pear, like a woman, still unopened in a bowl.

On the road to Damascus, St. Paul was blinded.
Then, he could see.

THE CAPTAIN OF VICE

wears gray trousers and a .35 caliber
handgun. A prostitute props herself
on the erotic corner of his desk, says,
in a fish-net voice, *I want to go straight,*
which means I want to stop vomiting
and hooking and having seizures.
She is metallic and acne. What is not
hot pink is lavender and white. Eclipse
of the downtrodden. Stare and go blind.
The Captain is Roman Catholic, choir-boy
and pure love. He carries a pyx,
holds the body of Christ
nestled in his hands. Cold blessings
he delivers to the sick in his spare time.
And she is sick, this same girl who shoots up,
who unzips dick for a living, is making fun of his
fat daughter, tells him how she beats her up, how
she makes her wet her pants. The Captain looms
over the hooker, misdemeanor criminal about to go free,
says nothing. He has his own battles: Johnny Walker Red,
a dead son, a brother drowned, a passenger
beheaded by windshield glass. *Enough,* he tells her,
take your ass home. And her ass, covered with pustules
sticking to her pants, spotted with tainted blood,
wiggles out the front door. She glances back at him.

HUMAN-HEADED BULL BELOW EMPTY SPACE

I.

On the lapis cylinders from 2900 BC images of the domestic
and the wild wrestle demons and musical instruments.
A human-headed bull braces a dulcimer while a bear plays and a fox
nestles at their feet. From *my* life, one scene inscribed
like that, so for twenty years a girl appears and reappears
in dreams. I am a young nurse, crisp uniform, high polished shoes,
carrying specimens that must be dropped off, when,
in the late after-hours of a cancer center, I get turned around.
I am lost somewhere in radiology. In each darkened room, huge
machinery and radioactive danger signs. Just minutes before,
on the ward where I worked, I massaged the feet of a boy
with testicular cancer. I rubbed his arch, and on a sketch pad
he drew my hands with charcoal. Precise lines he smeared
with his thumb. *You know, I just thought I was bigger*
than the other boys in gym class, he said, and added his own feet
to the drawing of my hands. Now the night has stopped itself
in this hall, and in my memory of him, the air is all enormous
cathedral. I turn left, and see a girl, whose back is to me,
standing before the new ultra-modern scanner, alone, arms outstretched,
her blue and white striped hospital robe, too large for her shoulders,
has fallen, and her hair, which I know will soon fall out, is luscious
and just barely reaches her hip. I watch her for how beautiful she is,
for how faithful she is to her position there, her arms held exactly,
for how she could be anyone, for how she could be me. The technician
arrives, directs me, directs her, and I resume the pace of someone found.
Some nights I dream I am photographing her, or painting her. And now
that I have seen the treasures of Ur, I dream I am carving her body
onto a lapis cylinder, then rolling her onto parchment.
She is my link to a moment still before me in my life, before
I had cleaned the body of my father newly dead. A moment in which
who I am is variable. I might have been the bear making music,

or the obedient human-headed bull supporting heavy strings.
But I have been frozen again. Mesmerized by my father's freckled skin,
as I turn him to place below him a clean sheet
one the funeral workers can take with them. I love the way his vacant
    mouth
accepts his false teeth, I touch the black sores on both heels,
and the yellow, tobacco stained nails of his right hand.
I carve the sight of him on my retina, roll him
across my cornea, his arms, like hers, once reaching out, now folded.
And I know, because I have never forgotten *her*, that this moment with
    him will last,
just the two of us, in the middle of the night, before I call anyone
to help. I sit down for awhile, slide my hand under his, and watch.

II.

Because now I have raised her up. Because now I have laid him down.
I tell her story to a friend who writes.
Maybe he will want to take her, and I will be able to let go
the responsibility of her fate, which has tracked me through the years
like a lion. Or the boy, whose testicular tumor
grew to incorporate his brain. Instead, my friend tells me his vision:
a night when he watched a dog from his city window.
Framed by the building's edge and the alley's long line,
light from an unknown source, moon maybe, streetlight, this dog,
curled, was reduced to *form*, his head and tail equal and still.
He remembers. I remember. The dog as girl as my father as a boy
as witness. Obedience and repose. My father *is* a dog a girl a boy
a human-headed bull falling below empty space, and it occurs to me,
that it is *this* which held us, *this* is what haunts, how we both saw,
for a moment, the empty space we are destined to fall through.

MISTAKES

My father's lips are the flat blue of the North Atlantic.
We stand at the terrace door in ordinary gray light,
watch men paint yellow lines across the parking lot's rows.
His chest rises, all air squeezed
between thin lips, he wants to talk about a mistake he made,
right there, at the corner of Fourth and Erie –
an old Jewish man and a black man
left the Colgate-Palmolive factory at 5 p.m. in one car –
the black man at that time, a *Negro*, the ride home
a political statement –
and my father saw them, saw
a truck cross the intersection, saw the car hit the side
of the truck, saw the black man, in slow motion rise
from his unrestrained seat, rise through
the windshield, then fall back into the seat,
his head landing outside on the hood,
and then remarkably, spinning to face his split body.

The mistake my father made
was in approaching the old Jewish man,
stunned in the driver's seat, in not shielding him,
who was, by all intents and circumstances, unhurt.
He allowed the old man time in which he might turn
to his passenger, turn
to ask him if he was all right,
turn first to the flailed neck,
then to the hood where the head had rested and spun,
and in that moment, the old man died from fright,
from the shock of it all.

Now, my hand on the hull of my father's back,
I can feel through the shirt cotton, his lungs
rasp and wheeze. With my other hand, I touch the tumor

buried below his left clavicle. Once it was a small lettuce,
ribbed and immovable, now it is melted, spurned,
responding, the doctor says. Hope is a third person in the room
as we watch sudden rain pound the parking lot,
pound the men as they run, leaving buckets of bright paint,
the pails overflow their liquid suns on tar,
eclipse the orderly lines, as now, my father
rests his hand over mine. *Let me tell you something,*
he says, *even small mistakes can haunt you.*

RITUAL, MY FATHER

Every night I soak, then rub his feet.
Their soles are cruel and blue, the arches flat.

I raise their cracked lengths to my knees.
Every night I soak, then rub his feet.

We have learned to sit still with his disease,
a task takes shape, within the fear, in that

every night I soak, then rub his feet,
their soles are cruel and blue, the arches flat.

BURNING

My mother said her lungs were on fire.
At times she actually called out *fire, fire.*
Flames rose up from the center of her dress.
They orbited her frame.
When she died, her rosary beads were prisms
in her hands. They made a flame in the casket.

My father sits in his favorite chair.
The parking lot across the street
fills the room with an icy blue light.
Over and over he turns to the couch.
I can't stop seeing your mother there,
he says. His face is ashy and expectant.

MORTUARY WORKERS

After we had cared for you so fanatically:
clean underpants, your false teeth set just right,
your hair combed so strangers would know we loved you,
after all our attempts to present you
as beloved, honored,
the funeral workers came in maroon sweat suits
to get you. This is the kind of joke you would like.
They were – *thugs* is the only word for it –
dressed like bookies, numbers men,
they were lifting you onto a narrow stretcher,
a plank of red rubber suspended on metal bars and wheels.
They were classic hit men from Secaucus,
characters from a topless bar, cigar men.
I thought I would lose my mind seeing them take you.
But I didn't, and by the next night
at McCloughlin's, they were quite formal,
ushering in the bereaved, the old friends.

I was in the middle of my own ceremony
surrounded by buffoons, and ex-cops,
and genuine well-wishers.
I was five and you were sitting on the floor,
I was leaning on your knee
rubbing my eyes,
and you were supporting the back of my neck,
as you continued to do my whole life,
holding me in place against your kind body,
you and I – secretly saying good-bye –
in a circus of velvet chairs, visitors, and gladioli.

NIGHT VISITOR, WINTER

I explore grief by drawing
    a white boat
on a navy blue horizon.

The moon is a radiographic breast,
    your scar, a wild horse
across its icy, veined outline.

The sky is a mathematical chart,
    angled, and the grief boat,
this thin vessel breaks open.

One night.

Then, months later, a second night –
the air sits beside me on the bed.
It is your weight, Mother,
    across my knees
and I am a white, shining boat.

On my breast, no, on my *moon*,
    your love for me gallops.

The sky's mathematical puzzle:
    you: not here: here.

EASTER

Parishioners dip hard-boiled eggs in red
until they sheen, luscious with sacrifice.

We glisten the eggs with olive oil.

This cave, this egg where my father lives, yolk-hard, blued,
is about to crack open – is about to spill resurrection.

Sorrow of the rectory's dark window.

My father is propped in an egg closet,
is laid out in the cave's eggy dark.

Night cracks the world.

We balance an egg in the spoon's cool mouth, lift it from the cup,
dip it in oil, until we are giddy with salvation.

In the first egg, my father's red hair.

In the second, his hand on my head.
In the third, a procession of palm crosses, my original purple sin.

My mother is on the corner in a dramatic yellow hat.

God is a hard-boiled decision-maker.
My father falls in the closet. This time
I save him. Other times, I can not save him.

THEN

Everything is about time and my father standing at eight years in the yard
    when his father was coming home, coming across the street, and it was all
about timing – the car and his father
    and my father's life turned into a place where he had no shoes no clothes
his mother suddenly never home cleaning offices in Manhattan

    about the time when he sees my mother, also eight, in a pretty dress
and carelessly swinging an empty bucket of clam chowder filled at the docks
    and she, not hungry like he and his younger brothers
swinging and letting some fall to the street.

    About that time he would say he immediately loved her
and she said he sang solo in Latin in the choir
    and she admired how clean he was even though everyone knew he was poor
he always had a crease in his pants and for a long time
    for the rest of their lives
he found things about her that he admired;
    she found things about him that made her proud. She wore seamed
stockings in three inch heels all day even when she was pregnant, even when she
    was walking us in a baby carriage. She would go with him to baseball card
shows where they would hold hands.

It was about the time they took us to Cooperstown to see the baseball Hall
    of Fame because we were always – *always* – in the nosebleed seats
and keeping score and flipping cards on the stoop for pennies and on the way
    my father bought me Bullfinch's Mythology, *Read this, you'll like it,* he said
and I did, of course, and the whole time was great there was a lake and all
    the baseball
stuff and my parents sitting on the porch of the little rooms like the powerful
gods and goddesses in my book which had me all excited
    and reading out loud to my brother;

    and it was about this time that the doctor said my brother's tumor
had probably started and so it was our last family vacation ever.

The next five years were like time as a blur and in the blur time so
    suddenly *precarious* and *precious*
and notice how close those words are to each other – well, I hadn't –
not before the time when my brother died, but after, well of course,
    though somehow
my parents still could be like gods and goddesses but with tragic flaws.

                        ≈

My mother's face was so sad like my father's face when he was eight
and she saw herself in him
    and he was careless and flinging everything they had saved – money
and plans – just like she had tossed the clam chowder
    and in that arc they saw themselves again.

        It was then that we relaxed back into our habits:
    reading and working and phoning each other from all over the
        country
with memories of *the time when* and *the time when*
    and we were in the biggest story of our lives, corny to say it
but a really happy family. It was about that time

                    my mother said she couldn't breathe
and eventually never did catch her breath; years later when she died
    my father went to Ireland where they had been so happy.
He heard there was an Irish poet whose books were hard to find
    and so in the rain and chill wind he walked really fast in his new
        sneakers
to a bookstore in Dublin and bored the clerk with stories about the
    time we went to
    Cooperstown and he bought me <u>Bullfinch's Mythology</u> and how that
changed my life forever
    how after that all he ever bought me was books and he brought home
everything the Irish poet had ever written – which was a lot of books –

                        28

he described walking back to the hotel and feeling the first twinge
in his chest – the first hint of the thing that would grow and make a
        shadow
    on his face that reminded him he said of how he'd looked – *haunted* –
        in the mirror that time when his father went flying into the air
in front of him – flying and then landing

                and how he imagines sometimes what my brother
was thinking when he went flying into the air and I said *don't, Dad*
    and about this time I said *Mommy will help you* and then he said
Jeez, there she is, and smiled and relaxed back into his body;
    recovered the eight-year-old body at that moment before his father
        died
while his mother was standing behind him in the gate waving to his father
    so that his father walked in front of the car

                and my father recaptured that face –
that face just before his father was hit, when he was waving, and
        everything –
    and I mean *everything* - was before him.

III

SNAKE

We are speeding through Georgia, your hand
between my legs in an orange VW Rabbit.

I am ashamed of the car and nothing else.
A black snake swims in the mirage of steam

over the tar road. If I let go my body
will plummet, so I am shifting in the seat

trying to hold onto your hand, to all of it.
My fingers are in your hair, we are

suspended like that when the frogs in the swamp
start their murderous squeals. I am mud.

I am lifting out of the car, the smell of pulp
from the mill like the smell of roaches all around us

and yet, I inhale, and lift, and hold the dashboard
like I am in a skiff, rising against the river.

Snake of my spine shimmers, splits the bones.
I loved you for that. For my dissolution, for my slither.

BODY

for Mike

I was a singer for you. I dressed in antique peach dresses with dozens
of buttons, and carved pears into juicy commas. I had a romantic vision,
but you were covered in camouflage paint that made a sick green
      of the bath water.
Your fingers were so cracked from rope exercises, that the buttons on
the old dress were a nuisance. Still, we could lie most nights, pressed
and resting on each other, sturdy and full, both of our bodies,
and talk about one day, talk about the next day.
                            Now in the house where I live alone,
the moon makes a hard light on the porch. Not a single leaf
on the tree this May. *Unusual,* everyone keeps saying,
but the barren rims of everything remind me how things continue
until they somehow don't continue, about the surprise
of things like car accidents, and paralysis. About how in an instant,
the body I could lean into, all of me, leaning into all of you,
could actually vanish. How the body becomes a chore, a thing
to position, like the painter positions the full-hipped woman
on brocade pillows. In the painting, as in the vacant life,
a woman leans on cushions as though they are the man she loves.

ATTACHMENT

after Rachel Contreni Flynn

I live in a town fastened to a field.
And it is the only thing I am attached to:
the wild grasses of a lot for sale.

I moved here from a town fastened to a mountain.
The air was upside down in the valley. Unbreathable.

Before that I lived in a city fastened to itself.
Every night stone and steel were lit from inside
until I saw Manhattan as a field, as a mountain.

In the big blackout, when I was twelve, I remember
all the shadows holding flashlights.

My fear dissipated in that dark,
as now, the field which holds my town in check to the South,
fills with furious gnats.

The field reminds me of my mother.
Her heart is open and dark.
Her skin is shimmering glass.

I live in a town like many towns,
and when I look up from the center of it,
I look into unexpected space, where grass, and little
white buds are busy.

Night is not an acrobat falling into a net.
Night is smoke, rising like a lover's hips into the dark.

NIGHT IS NOT AN ACROBAT FALLING INTO A NET

Night is not a door.
Night is not a shaman with burned herbs.

If night was an acrobat, it wouldn't use a net,
it would have nothing to be afraid of.

But night is afraid,
in the same way I am afraid.

Night is not the falling sky in the Chicken Little story,
nor is it blue music.

Sometimes night is as colorful as a tomato,
and bleeds in the window.

When I was a child, night was also a child.

Night is inside me, warm and filled with gnats,
day is also inside, but both have failed me.

When I was in love I waited for it, like I waited for rats
on the roof, with a terrible excitement:

I was in love in the South, in Savannah, where night is a river
that swirls and is murky and has snakes and pestilence.

We moved in that humid, moving dark
against our own hot skin, and slithered and cricketed our legs.

We fell awkwardly into night, like the acrobats we were not.
And night received us, like the rainy circus it was.

WHO DIES OF THIRST

On my desk the dahlia is a fisted door,
is a feather falling between myself and the man I am trying to help:
train-jumper, *transient*. After three days in the Thompson Falls jail
his body's rancid scent overwhelms me. He is a criminal trespasser.

I go with an escort to his trailer, which straddles a ravine.
The rusted shell explodes with mice, attracts
a red-winged hawk. The sky is a berth behind the circling
hawk, I escape for a moment in the wing's spiked tip.
We leave medicines, lift the wire fence back in place.

I latch the day. Across the road a spitting llama
rolls in pink flowers. Inside, in my gut, a cramp
of what I no longer want to give away.
I am tired of serving people.

I believed I would live like Kateri Tekawitha.
Disfigured, she leaned over the parched lips of Indians,
caught in their blistering smallpox.

I would rise everyday into goodness, place
cool cloths on foreheads, make pumices
and plasters, and then at death,
like hers, my scars would rapturously fade.

I would ascend, luminescent.
This was the wildflower story I was living in.

But my back gave out from lifting bodies in their beds,
from leaning over the colostomy's rosy stoma.
I resented the way people held on to me, in labor,
in death. I saw birth as a *tearing away* of flesh.

I carried my imagined *real life* in a metal cart strapped
to my ankles. Everywhere I looked: faces,
when all I wanted was the empty desert.

Red rock of the free life.
Carved wall of the vacant cave.
I ate delicious words when I was alone.
What will I be if I am not a caretaker? My hands
are flat expressions of themselves, are unrecognizable.

This morning, an explosion of gnats and flies,
sweet maple window
drawing them to *this* life, as I am drawn to leave mine.
I call in sick
and fall into Salmon Lake
which has become a kind of room where green
is nothing more than a cool cool day.
Lake, open and rocky, my hands are returned to me
as they pass over lily pads and shift the silt
that coats dark water. The floating leaves are words,
words are bubbles that rise to the surface
circling my thighs. Words smell like pine.

The lake is a velvet confessional,
I kneel in its arms. The lake is thought, and memory.
In the water, my dead brother rises clean of agony,
and we are watching art slides after school
with my father. Our knees touch in the dark
as we practice dry, innocent kisses on our hands.
The lake is the gold parlor of my childhood.
The lake is a book. The lake is my first lover,
my best lover. The lake is the moon we thought we would colonize.
The lake is the colony we named Lorca.

In the distance a siren heads down Highway 83,
and the sound of a child falling sounds like a child
falling away. The day moves from east to west over water.

Can I be left in my cool lake?
Can I *be* the cool lake?

LAKE, BODY

1.

Once my body was a wave, was all water
and I was rising and crashing
and in my rising and crashing the thready seaweed
was something my lover could taste
and the ropes of my muscles
were like barrels marking *danger*
in the surf. I saved him,
my body was as salty as a wave
was invisible and dark green and curling.

2.

Because this is all so fresh in my mind,
this life where I was a Sea,
something about your voice
pulls me out of the earth I am living in,
pulls me like a root up from my complacency –
singes my skin, tears open the skin which has its own locks
and doors
and out from the door I come weeping
for what I have lost: muscles like ropes, pink waves,
the lover's way of looking at me,
the lover.

3.

It sounds like nostalgia but it is not.
It sounds like music but it is heroin in a spoon.
It sings of going away,
all the words in the song are about going away.

4.

Something about the lake makes a whole in the world
that has poppies as big as oranges in it,
the room as cozy as my mother's lap
or the map of my father's hands. That *something*
comes in around the windows.

We are in Maine. It might be a vacation
except I am splitting open,
except I am leaping out of my skin into the room.
I say the words that terrify me even in my sleep: *alone, undesirable.*
Then I stop speaking and a lavender spider (*miracle*) walks
from my fourth vertebra into the room.

5.

In one picture my brother and I have our hands out,
and a pony is lifting sugar from our palms
with his substantial tongue. In another picture
St. Francis of Assisi has turned from his bible
to spread his hands out, unfurled
towards the vast desert and a light
which is the tongue of God has descended.

So one way to be saved is through the light,
and one way to be saved is by the pony
who licks us after the sugar cube is gone
who licks our hands for the memory
of something luscious and sweet.

6.

I am a wave.
The briny light has come for me.
The lover has not disappeared
but is lost in the mountains.
My parents are gone, my brother is gone.

I may go with a posse to find them,
Or I may just turn from the position of going away,
turn to face the lover,
find a way to re-enter the Sea,
a way to lay my hand
on the spinning blade of a heart.

FIRE

All the world lives in a ball of fire
that grows out of steel and glass.

During the Vietnam War, my father wrote prayers
on index cards that he taped over my bed.

I said novenas because I liked the ritual:
nine days reciting from the missal
with a sewn-in statue of the Infant of Prague.

His heart, wrapped in thorns, was bleeding.

Last night I stood at the window and practiced dying.

And then I lay back down,
spread my arms out and crossed my feet at the arch
and remembered to open my palms upward.

For the first time in three months I didn't dream of fire.

I dreamed of a friend who works for peace.
I was making a collage box for him,
the black paper I was cutting
was the night sky,
there were fish in the sky,
and words in Latin over my head.

Blessed are the peacemakers, someone was saying,
maybe it was God
or maybe it was my father,
I don't know, but it repeated itself in the dream
until I believed I was living again
in a booming, beautiful world.

SHAMES, ALSO LOVE

after James Merrill

1. Boredom:

In my softest robe, I talk to myself,
the photos on the wall more alive than I am.
In one, my friend leaps from a cliff, suspended in the air and naked,
all his years as a soldier outlined in the muscles of his belly.

What happens when he lands will be:
a race to the water, a splashing dive, deep kisses underwater.
Then, over time he disappears and I am left in the cupped dune:
high wild grass and in it, a dead seal, formless.
Its small head fades into a wide, intact body,
all that made it *seal* is vanished.

All of us: myself, the lover, the seal,
once held our bodies in clean dives over water.
Now I hold my head to my knees, *Where is that life?*
The bed's hypnotic trap door gives way.
Not sleep exactly, but falling.

2. Fear:

I recognize it as an old friend in vintage clothes –
we embrace – all the talk of rats and snakes.
Predictable terror.
In the narrow alley, she sabotages me,
wraps fat around my belly, around my sagging upper arms.
She makes an indoors of the body,
shows me the limits of doors and locks.
She says, Stay hidden.
Outside the killers are. Outside the lovers are.

3. Mixed Vanities and Shames:

My lover has eaten an orange.
When he enters, camouflage paint and sweat,
his fingers taste of juice.
I live a long time in the zesty flavor of his calf.
All the things I want to do to him are lined up like jarred fruit.
Behind the tight, vacuumed glass:
luscious ways to enter him.
Waking, shame for what was lost.
Not the lover's exit; it was his job to come and go.
No *body shame* in all the shattered jars
and winter just beginning.

4. Also Love:

I was an anemic child with stiff necks,
a spastic colon and a propensity for love and affection.
I was unprepared for the death of my brother
who wasted into nothingness.
I knew his skin better than my own.

In its dry pouch, my heart skipped beats, nearly stopped.
I understand Dr. White's obsession with fungus.
I watch her sneak cultures from the newly dead:
aspergillosis, candida albicans.
The tissues already blackened and split.
I practice the ceremony of post-mortem care.
The act of washing the dead,
their spirits still in a swirl at the belly button,
exiting as all devoted breath withdraws.

This practice of studying abandoned bodies –
seal or lover or stranger –
is also a practice of love.

SOURCE

From the bed raised high to the window: white and maple.
A neighbor smoking on the back porch cups his hands to his face,
and walks in circles hitting shrill wind chimes.

Today I have space. No glass. The September fireball now only
occasionally wakens. Maybe once a week I see the falling day.

I drive the road to the Bison Range, it is a Sunday, just after the New Year.
A hawk takes a duck, its talons spear white, and they skim,
body-heavy, together, across the hood of my car. A spot of red grows

on the feathery belly, and the duck's wings: inadequate, clumsy
have blocked my view for just a moment, have managed to suspend
        them both
before my car, so that for days I remember the claw, and the call, and
        the blood.

I could say this is the source of my sadness but it would be a lie.

IV

BODY PARABLE

I.

I make a cave of the body.
Nightly, bats hang in a communion of sleep.
Their tiny faces – shadowy triangles
of fallen angels.

It suffices, it suffocates.
I am tucked in, tucked beneath the lover's skin.

II.

I was pale, foliate.
My skin a fragile parchment, so even in my crib
my bones, pressing from the inside
made red circles on pressure points.

I started to see my body as *the other*,
pallor of the stranger I woke to each morning,
shuffling in leggings and velvet helmet hats with tassels,
the well-dressed child
with ailments, swollen glands, and a barking cough.

Dog body.

I would press my thumb nail under my index nail
until the little moons bled.

III.

My brother was a tan and limber miracle.
He let me borrow his healthy skin,
I could run alongside him, alongside

the furnace of his body.
Leisure of him. Deliberate.
If I hung as a bat then,
I hung from his sturdy body.

Shelter the bat, shelter the dog-child, she is anemic,
she is talking about herself as *the other*,
he is saving her.

IV.

Imagine the world when he is taken from me.

V.

Farmhouse in the mountain's muddy side,
back room, loud music,
my body under a boy's body, cold brick wall as bed.

In each of the twenty-four window panes
a tiny reflection of our flesh: marbled, clamorous fucking.
I searched his musty lap and pubis
for my own desire.

I found instead the coal of my spine
and a kind of temporary heat.
Stoked.
Stroked.
Cleaved.

In the backyard crows flew up in ashy chaos.
The black cows were an ache on the hill,
gnashing burnt grass.
I inspected bruises with satisfaction.
A kind of living it was, a kind of leaving it was.

VI.

Happiness keeps its eyes shut.
Except one day Mike's knee touched my knee.
We were on the Savannah River in an adequate boat,
outboard motor. The rocking sun.
I found everything in his knee, like a scavenger hunt,
I entered the world there.

I entered the scar on the back of his head.
I entered his thighs, they seemed as wide as a horse's back,
sky-wide, hard rock of entering, cold wall collapsing.
All body fluids as delicious as pear juice.
His embrace was all lather and sharp knife,
his kisses all fume and immaculate fuel.

Exculpatory furnace. Love, the unexpected, incessant
chatter of our bodies.
Was I still a bat? I hung upside down in him.
Was I still a dog? I was as faithful as a happy Labrador.

VII.

My body was a beloved chore.
My body was a mischievous pirate.
My body flew over the lover, it was a holiday, it was religion.
My body was fluent in eleven languages, it painted
frescoes with my tongue, and stood like St. Francis
at the cliff edge, imploring no end to this happiness,
calling out for redemptive forgiveness.
I remember there were crows in ashy clouds,
and cows on the hill, some standing,
some kneeling down.
I remember making love vigorously, caw-cawing,
barking, mooing.

I touched his knee,
his semen stained the sheets,
it was as translucent and as luminous as the moon.

My body collapsed under the phone call of his accident.
That's two, I remember thinking.

He took his place alongside my lost brother, and I took back
my bat wings, my clear, extended ears.
I took back my furry solitude.

VIII.

I wake in the winter of my forty-fifth year, in a room
with a black metal vase, white branches fingering the shade,
and I have grown fat; I have become an unrecognizable other.

My nipples can still be militant and joyous.

And I imagine I may have to fly out into the sun, risking everything.

But I am afraid to leave the cave.
And I am equally afraid of the cave's tremulous walls.

There is a moment when the bat drops from the pearly, moist dome
before there is room enough for flight –

this is the moment I am living in:

my body is falling away from the story of my body.

Notes

"Lake, Body" is for Joseph E. Myer.

"Human-Headed Bull Below Empty Space" is after a story by David Rutschman.

The line *Happiness keeps its eyes shut,* in "Body Parable" is from *Analects,* by Paul Valery.

"Fire" is inspired by Harold Shapiro's work for peace in the Middle East.

The Irish poet in "Then" is Ciaran Carson.

The Author

Mary Jane Nealon received her MFA from Warren Wilson College. She is the recipient of two fellowships from The Fine Arts Work Center in Provincetown, and awards from the Mid-Atlantic Arts Foundation, the New Jersey State Council on the Arts, and the Poetry Society of America. She is the Amy Lowell Poetry Traveling Scholar for 2004-2005. She lives in Missoula, Montana.